The Resume and Cover Letter Writing Toolkit for the $uccessful Job Seeker

Learn to Write Resumes and Cover Letters that Hiring Authorities Want to Read to Help You Get Hired Faster!

Oreste J. D'Aversa

PUBLISHER'S NOTE

This book is designed to provide accurate and authoritative information in regard to the subject matter covered. It is sold with the understanding that neither the author nor publisher is engaged in rendering psychological, legal or other professional service. If psychological, legal, professional advice or other expert assistance is required, the services of a professional, in that field, should be sought. The principles and concepts presented in this book are the opinions of the author and based on his interpretations of the aforementioned principles. Neither the author nor publisher is liable or responsible to any person or entity for any errors contained on this book, website, or for any special, incidental, or consequential damage caused or alleged to be caused directly or indirectly by the information contained on this book or website. Any application of the techniques, ideas and suggestions in this book is at the reader's sole discretion and risk.

Copyright © Oreste J. D'Aversa, 2021. All rights reserved.

No part of this publication may be reproduced, redistributed, taught, stored in a retrieval system, or transmitted, in any form or by any means, electronic, mechanical, photocopy, recording, or otherwise, without the prior written permission of the publisher.

FIRST EDITION

ISBN: 978-1-95-229424-2

Published by: *Cutting Edge Technology Publishing*.

Table of Contents

1. About the Author 5
2. Introduction 7
3. Purpose of the Resume 11
4. Action Verbs 13
5. OARS - Objective/Action/Result/Statement 19
6. Components of the Resume 23
7. Sample Resumes 33
8. Worksheets 43
9. Cover Letters 57
10. Cover Letter Template 59
11. Sample Cover Letters 61
12. Conclusion 65
13. If You Want to Post Your Resume 67

NOTES

1. About the Author

Oreste J. D'Aversa is a Job Search Coach and has worked with hundreds of people to help them find new and better jobs. Delivering real world experience as a former Executive Recruiter and Human Resources Manager.

Mr. D'Aversa is also business owner, Business Coach, Consultant, Trainer, Author, Public Speaker, University Lecturer and Advisor to Senior Management, providing Strategic Planning, Consulting and Training services to, Small Businesses, Entrepreneurs, Salespeople and other Consultants.

He has appeared on radio and television to discussing his books on professional and personal development.

He is author of the following books:

- *The Resume Writing Kit*
- *SELLING for NON-SELLING Professionals*
- *SELL More Technology NOW! Proven Sales Methods and Established Practices that Deliver Results*
- *Life Beyond The Pandemic: A Practical New Journey Handbook*
- *(all available on Amazon.com).*

He can be reached at:

Oreste J. D'Aversa, Owner

Metropolitan Small Business Coaching LLC

www.MetroSmallBusinessCoaching.com

eMail:OresteDAversa@outlook.com

NOTES

2. Introduction

The Resume, the foundation of your job search. The basic marketing tool for those seeking employment. Your Resume is your brochure featuring you as the product and separating you apart from others when looking for a job!

Did you know that most Resumes are only reviewed for about <u>10 to 14 seconds</u> by hiring authorities?

The purpose of this document is to teach you how to skillfully prepare your Resume to get the attention of hiring authorities and executive recruiters. You want to understand what **<u>they</u>** are looking for, so **<u>you</u>** get the call for an interview. It is also especially important to understand that the Resume and interview process is about what **<u>you can do for your prospective employer</u>** and not what they can do for you. It becomes all about **<u>you</u>** when you get the job offer!

That's why it's important that your Resume be clear, concise, and demonstrates your achievements as to get the reader's attention as soon as possible so that the reader <u>calls you</u> for an interview!

Think of Your Resume as:

- Your Calling Card
- A Door Opener
- A Statement of Your Competencies
- A Marketing Brochure Featuring You as the Product

WHY A CANDIDATE'S RESUME IS ELIMINATED FROM CONSIDERATION

- Resume is too long—it contains too many details (rarely more than 2 pages)//
- It rambles—the information is not organized and/or it is poorly formatted
- Overselling yourself: the "I can do everything" or "I will do anything approaches
- Typos, grammatical errors, misspelled words
- Use of gimmicks (odd paper colors, fonts, paper shapes and sizes—use of photo)
- Evidence of too much: "Job Hopping" without legitimate reasons
- Employment gaps not explained
- Too much about what you want—not enough about what you can do for the employer
- Incomplete information regarding: Work History, Experience Skills, Achievements, and Education
- Use of adverbs and too many qualitative adjectives (should be quantitative when used)
- Achievement statements that begin with "Responsible for" or "weak verbs" such as: aided, participated in, involved with, helped—these merely imply that you were there!

NOTES

3. Purpose of the Resume

What is the real purpose of a Resume? You may think the purpose of a Resume is to get you a job. In truth, a well prepared resume **gets you an interview** and an interview gets you a job. People hire people not Resumes!

What should be on your Resume? The content of your Resume is important to help you get that phone call for that all important interview.

The Different Styles of Resumes:

Chronological

Functional

Combination

The style most accepted and used in today's marketplace is the Chronological format. This format will be the focus in The Resume Writing Kit. The Functional and Combination Resume, though used, are frowned upon by hiring authorities and executive recruiters. The main reason is that these types of Resumes are difficult to read and understand.

They do have their place in the job search but should be used with caution. Should you like to learn more about Functional Resumes I suggest you go to your public library or perform research on the Internet.

NOTES

4. Action Verbs

Employers hire people who can perform skilled tasks for them. Your Resume should be written to clearly and concisely communicate the message that you possess valuable skills. Your future employer is extremely interested in your accomplishments. If you have accomplished work objectives in the past, chances are you will be a strong contributor to your new employer in the future.

You want to demonstrate to the reader that you played an **active** role in your career and were not a spectator who watched from the sidelines.

Look at the following statement and choose the stronger word. "*Assisted* the Human Resources Department in writing the employee handbook", **OR** "*Collaborated* with the Human Resources Department in writing the employee handbook". *Assisted* sounds like you supplied paper for the copy machine while *Collaborated* infers you were working shoulder to shoulder with Human Resources Department to construct the employee handbook.

The following list of verbs, by no means complete, and is a good place to start your search for strong action verbs/words to describe what you have accomplished.

Adapted	Designed	Investigated	Protected
Advised	Developed	Judged	Questioned
Administered	Diagnosed	Learned	Read
Analyzed	Directed	Lectured	Reasoned
Applied	Discovered	Led	Recommended
Approved	Displayed	Listened	Reconciled
Arranged	Drew	Located	Recorded
Assembled	Edited	Maintained	Recruited
Assessed	Encouraged	Managed	Reduced
Assisted	Estimated	Measured	Reinforced

Balanced	Established	Mediated	Reorganized
Budgeted	Evaluated	Memorized	Repaired
Classified	Expedited	Mentored	Reported
Clarified	Followed	Monitored	Researched
Coached	Forged	Motivate	Restored
Collected	Formulated	Negotiated	Retrieved
Coordinated	Founded	Nurtured	Revised
Communicated	Gathered	Observed	Reviewed
Compared	Generated	Operated	Scheduled
Compiled	Guided	Organized	Shaped
Completed	Handled	Originated	Simplified
Computed	Helped	Participated	Solved
Conceived	Identified	Perceived	Spoke
Conceptualized	Implemented	Performed	Synthesized
Conducted	Improved	Persisted	Streamlined
Confronted	Improvised	Persuaded	Studied
Constructed	Increased	Planned	Supervised
Contrasted	Influenced	Prepared	Supported
Controlled	Initiated	Presented	Taught
Coordinated	Integrated	Processed	Tested
Comprehended	Inspired	Produced	Trained
Counseled	Installed	Programmed	Treated
Created	Instructed	Promoted	Tutored
Decided	Interpreted	Proposed	Validated
Defined	Interviewed	Proved	Volunteered

The Resume and Cover Letter Writing Toolkit for the $uccessful Job Seeker

| Demonstrated | Invented | Provided | Wrote |

SAMPLE ACTION VERBS LISTED BY FUNCTIONAL SKILL AREA

COMMUNICATION	CREATIVE	DETAILORIENTED	INVESTIGATING/RESEARCH
Aided	Acted	Analyzed	Calculated
Arbitrated	Abstracted	Approved	Catalogued
Advised	Adapted	Arranged	Collected
Clarified	Composed	Classified	Computed
Consulted	Conceptualized	Collated	Conducted
Contributed	Created	Compared	Correlated
Cooperated	Designed	Complied	Critiqued
Coordinated	Developed	Documented	Diagnosed
Counseled	Directed	Enforced	Discovered
Debated	Drew	Follow through	Examined
Defined	Fashioned	Met deadlines	Experimented
Directed	Generated	Prepared	Extrapolated
Enlisted	Illustrated	Processed	Evaluated
Explained	Imagined	Recorded	Gathered
Expressed	Improvised	Retrieved	Identified
Helped	Integrated	Set priorities	Inspected.
Influenced	Innovated	Systemized	Interpreted
Informed	Painted	Tabulated	Investigated
Inspired	Performed		Monitored
Interpreted	Planned		Observed
Interviewed	Problem solved		Organized

Mediated
Merged
Negotiated
Promoted
Recommended
Represented
Resolved
Suggested

Shaped
Synthesized
Visualized
Wrote

Proved
Reviewed
Surveyed
Tested

ORGANIZING	PROVIDING SERVICE	MANUAL SKILLS	FINANCIAL
Achieved	Advised	Arranged	Administered
Assigned	Attended	Assembled	Allocated
Administered	Cared	Bound	Analyzed
Consulted	Coached	Built	Appraised
Contracted	Coordinated	Checked	Audited
Controlled	Counseled	Classified	Budgeted
Coordinated	Delivered	Constructed	Calculated
Decided	Demonstrated	Controlled	Computed
Delegated	Explained	Cut	Developed
Developed	Furnished	Designed	Evaluated
Directed	Generated	Developed	Figured
Established	Inspected	Droved	Maintained
Led	Installed	Handled	Managed
Negotiated	Issued	Installed	Performed
Organized	Mentored	Invented	Planned
Planned	Referred	Maintained	

Prioritized	Repaired	Monitored
Produced	Provided	Prepared
Recommended	Purchased	Operated
Reported	Submitted	Repaired
		Tested

NOTES

5. OARS - Objective/Action/Result/Statement

It's all about accomplishments. What have you done for anyone lately?

The **OARS** formula will help you describe to the reader your professional accomplishments.

O - The business **OBJECTIVE** (problem, challenge, etc.) for which you were responsible to perform.

A - The **ACTION** you took to solve the business objective usually begins with an *ACTION VERB* (See section).

R - What was the **RESULT** that you obtained measured in some type of quantifiable terms (saved or made a company money, saved time, increased productivity, reduced costs, etc.)?

S - The **STATEMENT** you put together from the above three items.

OARS Accomplishment Statement:

Objective + Action + Result = Statement

RESULTS MAY BE EXPRESSED IN:

Dollars – Percentages – Work Hours – Ratios – Quotas - People

Money Saved – Money Earned

Time Saved – Process Improved

Winning Back Lost Customers

Improving Morale to Increase Productivity

OR

Improving Morale to Reduce Employee Turnover

Did You Meet or Exceed:

Deadlines, Budgets,
Expectations, Goals, and Objectives

Did You Increase:

Productivity, Customer Satisfaction,
Market Share, Efficiency, Effectiveness, Customer Retention,
Morale, New Business, and Quality

Did You Decrease:

Turnaround Time, Cycle Time, Down Time,
Problems, Waste, Debt, Back Log, Inventory, Man Hours,
Employee Turnover, Accounts Payable,
Product or Service Costs, Customer Complaints

The following **OARS** Statements are examples from Resumes. Good **OARS** Statements use action verbs. The order is not so important as to all items (Objective/Action/Result) are identified.

1. **Increased** sales through new prospects and installed base accounts, expanding sales by 30%.

2. **Created** and **conducted** interview training program for managers reducing candidate interview process by 25%.

3. **Implemented** order processing system which increased efficiency in the customer service department when interfacing with clients.

NOTES

6. Components of the Resume

The components of the Resume should include:

- Heading

- Summary (Professional or Executive)

- Work History with Achievements

- Professional Development/Additional Skills

- Education

In this section there will be a discussion of each **Component of the Resume** with examples to illustrate their usage.

Heading

The **Heading** section contains your contact information: name, address, telephone numbers with area code and e-mail address. It is very important that potential employers and recruiters are able to contact you. Make sure your contact information is accurate and you have voicemail or other methods of receiving your messages. It is a good practice, while you are in your job search, to make sure you have a professional sounding message on your voicemail.

John Smith   **212-555-1234**

100 Main Street, Anytown, State 12345   e-Mail: jsmith@hotmail.com

Summary

The **Professional Summary** section contains the main points of your professional qualifications. It is a snapshot of your experience, skills and work traits. It is a good place to start placing your **"keywords"** (words that are used by computer scanners/resume databases and hiring authorities). **Keywords** are skills and qualifications that indicate your professional abilities. The more keywords you have on your Resume the greater the chance your resume will be selected for review. The **Professional Summary** should contain no more than six (6) lines.

Below are two styles of writing the **Professional Summary**. Pick a style that you prefer. Remember that the purpose of the **Professional Summary** is to give the reader an overview of your professional skills and ability.

Professional Summary

A management consultant with extensive experience with project management, information technology and implementation of financial software solutions. Performed consulting for Fortune 500 clients and have expertise in; business analysis, requirement definition, technical design specifications and software evaluations. Organized, analytical, results-oriented and excellent interpersonal skills.

Professional Summary

A management consultant with extensive experience with project management, information technology and implementation of financial software solutions. Organized, analytical, results-oriented and excellent interpersonal skills.

Consulting	Programming	Mentoring
Keyword	Keyword	Keyword
Keyword	Keyword	Keyword

Both styles are acceptable. Some people prefer to work with one style over the other.

Professional Summary Examples

Corporate Administrative Assistant/Executive Secretary with extensive experience at the highest executive level. Major strengths in organization and detail, verbal and written communications and all aspects of managerial travel. Works independently. Exceptionally good judgment. A well-organized, dependable professional who takes pride in her work.

Senior Financial executive with wide-ranging experience at Fortune 10 Company and Big 6 accounting firm. Expertise includes strategic planning, budgeting, financial reporting, financial analysis & modeling, acquisitions/ divestitures, financial controls and project management. Innovative financial and operational problem-solver. Excellent interpersonal skills.

A Senior Management/Marketing Professional with experience building profits in a broad range of product and service businesses. Major strengths include strategic, customer focused, marketing management; creative problem solving; and excellent interpersonal skills. Organized, analytical, and results-oriented.

An Information Technology professional experienced with developing IBM's Customer Relationship Management (CRM) solutions on enterprise systems. Major strengths include problem solving skills and programming logic for mainframe applications. Ability to translate customer needs into technology solutions. Team player with ability to learn and apply new skills in a short amount of time.

Work History with Achievements

This section **Work History with Achievements** (or **Professional History** or **Professional Experience** or **Work History**) is presenting to the reader, your various employers, location of employment, dates of employment, responsibilities and accomplishments, in reverse chronological order, listing your most recent job first, then next job before that, then next job before that, etc.

This section supports and gives the reader the details of your **Summary**. This area is where you demonstrate your responsibilities and show your accomplishments, position by position, going back no more than twenty (20) years. Your reader is very concerned about your most recent position as those skills are currently being used and/or are fresh in your work history and to a lesser extent the positions and skills five (5) years before that and to a even lesser extent ten (10) years before that. Not to say that your work history is not important but the "perception" is that older positions and skills are not as current or "fresh" as your most recent position.

Work History with Achievements

Acme Inc., New York, New York 2000-2002

A Fortune 500 company specializing in telecommunications and technology.

Senior Marketing Director

Responsible for all marketing activities for northeast division and management marketing team.

- Implemented major accounts program under time and budget saving department 3 months and $100,000 in implementation services fees.

- Created nationwide marketing programs which aided sales team to generate $2 million dollars in revenue in 6 months.

- Analyzed marketing proposal work flow and created new policies and procedures resulting in faster turn-around times for proposals to sales team.

- **OARS Accomplishment: Objective + Action + Result = Statement**

Professional Development/Additional Skills

The section **Professional Development/Additional Skills** contains skills and training acquired in a non-academic environment (i.e., not in a University, College or High School). You may possess business skills and education that may be very valuable to your future employer, though not acquired in an academic environment, important none the less.

For example, you may have acquired computer skills on the job over a period of years. Or you have been trained in a certain sales methodology like "Miller-Heiman Strategic Selling".

Remember, only business-related skills and education, are what your future employer and recruiters are interested in. That's the additional value you bring to them.

Professional Development

Sales Training, Miller-Heiman – Strategic and Conceptual Selling

Meeting Planner, Certified Meeting Planner, American Planning Association

Seminar Leader, Certified Seminar Leader, American Seminar Leaders Association

Additional Skills

Computer Skills, Microsoft – Word, Excel, PowerPoint and Outlook

Foreign Language, Spanish – Read, Write, Speak

Notary Public, Licensed in State of New Jersey until June 2005

Education

The Education section is where your formal higher education (e.g. PhD, Master's, Bachelor's, and Associates Degree) is placed. Only completed degrees are to be mentioned. High school diploma can be shown if you have not had a college education.

Education

M.S., Engineering, SUNY – University of Albany

B.S., Business, Rutgers College

A.S., Computer Science, Nassau Community College

7. Sample Resumes

NOTES

John Smith   212-555-1212

100 Main Street, Anytown, State 12345   e-Mail: jsmith@hotttmail.com

SAMPLE CHRONOLOGICAL RESUME

PROFESSIONAL SUMMARY

General Manager and Senior Marketing Executive with an extensive record of achievement with Fortune 1000 companies including Information and Financial Services, Telecommunications and Consumer Products. Produces outstanding results through leadership, vision, organization development, communications, and strategic alliances and managing overall profitability.

PROFESSIONAL EXPERIENCE

Automatic Data Processing, Inc., Parsippany, New Jersey   1997-2001

Senior Director Marketing, eBusiness Services, Major Accounts Division

- Built and maintained key alliances instrumental in delivering innovative client solutions with minimal expense and reduced time to market.
- Developed and launched the Major Accounts portal, a comprehensive business to employee, web-based, self-service application targeted at mid-market employers and their employees. Currently in pilot in the Atlanta and Los Angeles regions.
- Launched a web-based travel and expense reporting and tracking application. Exceeded initial revenue and client acquisition targets.
- Introduced a voluntary employee, and payroll deduction insurance program in five key regions. Currently in phased national rollout.
- Created the Y2K client awareness and customer care education campaign. Achieved a "zero incidence" target.
- Developed the Valued Client Loyalty Program for the Miami and Dallas regions resulting in a $1.5M revenue gain in client retention over 18 months.

Nynex Long Distance Co., New York, New York   1996-1997

Assistant Vice President, Consumer Markets

- Developed the consumer market strategy and test launch of the Nynex Long Distance Company (NLD). Receive award for launching NLD on time and within budget strengthening the company's position in the Bell Atlantic merger.
- Identified ethnic and general market profiles resulting in focused communications and higher than expected direct response.
- Implemented a channel strategy lowering acquisition cost and expected consumer churn.

John Smith   212-555-1212

Western Union Financial Services, Paramus, New Jersey   1990-1996

Director, Development, 1992-1996
- Introduced the first pre-paid Phone Card resulting on $8M first year revenue.
- Developed a long-term plan to lower cost, increasing profitability over 18 months by $5M.
- Initiated process to identify new business opportunities, establishing a critical path, benchmarks, and selection and success criteria.

Product Manager, Consumer Money Transfer, 1991-1992
- Developed and executed business plan generating over $200M in revenue.
- Managed $20M budget for network and spot television, African American radio, local marketing, and market research.
- Developed over 250 customized key network volume building programs reversing a 13% decline in major markets to a 3% increase. Received the 1992 President's Award.

Product Manager, Message Services, 1990-1991
- Conducted market research among users, identifying key product weaknesses.
- Spearheaded strategy to re-position Telegram and improve product quality resulting in a 40% increase in Telegram delivery and a $.3M decrease in customer refunds.

Nabisco Brands, Inc., East Hanover, New Jersey
1985-1990

Marketing Manager, Biscuit Division, Snack Cracker Category, 1988-1990
- Introduced Harvest Crisps, the first national low fat, cholesterol and sodium free snack cracker. Achieved $25M in year one sales.
- Received 1990 Marketing Excellence Award for Best New Product Introduction.

Merck, Sharp & Dohme, West Point, Pennsylvania   1984
Market Research, Summer Intern

EDUCATION

MBA, Concentration in Marketing, June 1985
The Wharton School, University of Pennsylvania, Philadelphia, Pennsylvania

BA, Economics and French, Dean's List,
May 1980 Tufts University, Medford, Massachusetts

John Smith   212-555-1212

100 Main Street, Anytown, State 12345   e-Mail: jsmith@hotttmail.com

SAMPLE CHRONOLOGICAL RESUME
with Skills from Summary Highlighted

PROFESIONAL SUMMARY

A professional scientist with over ten year's experience in biochemical and pharmaceutical fields. Major strengths include methods development, research, analysis, and training. Precise, organized, and flexible.

Chemical analysis	R.M. testing	Implementation of Worksheet
Wet Chemistry	Formulation	Protein Purification
Method Development	Equipment Calibration	Production
Method Validation	Environmental Health	Engineering

PROFESSIONAL EXPERIENCE

Bausch and Lomb, Valley Cottage, NY   1994-2000
Research Scientist/Formulator

Performed methods development, stability studies, validated methods, and performed crossover studies. Trained staff on assay methodology and test instrument use. Selected as Environmental Health and Safety Coordinator.

- Created and introduced worksheet procedure to focus and facilitate FDA inspections of new drugs applications.
- Analyzed various color reformulations of smaller dosage Diamox Capsule, which increased differentiation versus generics and expanded international acceptance.
- Initiated a plan to get certified to calibrate and perform preventive maintenance on lab instruments, eliminating the cost of outsourcing.
- Established procedure to document training received by staff to facilitate FDA audits.
- Developed an improved method for SDS-PAGE, which eliminated "shadow" on the gels.
- Successfully trained, cross-trained, and managed a small group of analytical chemists while supervisor was out on maternity leave.

Pfizer Pharmaceuticals, Brooklyn, NY   1993-1994
Analyst

Tested raw materials, in-proc Tested raw materials, in-process and finished products using thin   layer chromatography.

- Increased efficiency of TLC testing by 33%, allowing HPLC and dissolution work to be done concurrently.

John Smith   212-555-1212

American Home Products, Pearl River, NY   1992-1993

Control Chemist

Analyzed raw materials using USP, NF and in-house test methods.

- Trained new employees and cross-trained chemists from different groups in wet chemistry, resulting in a 50% reduction of the 200-hour testing backlog within 4 months.

Purdue Frederick, Yonkers, NY   1991-1992

Assistant Scientist

Studied the performance of narcotic dosages and particularly evaluated the content, uniformity, stability, and dissolution of morphine.

- Performed calibration of HPLC systems to ensure GMP compliance.

Bayer Diagnostics, Tarrytown, NY   1985-1990

Biochemical Technician, 1987-1990

Purified and characterized antibodies in-house. Assayed liquid and dry blend reagents for blood analyzers and performed quality/stability testing of reagents and equipment to ensure all elements met specifications.

Product Engineering Technician, 1986

Developed techniques for extruding Teflon tubing of various dimensions for the CHEM-1 instrument and trained production technicians to prepare all tubing necessary to support CHEM-1 production.

Biochemical Technician, 1985

Performed pre-production scale up of processes to produce automated analyzer reagents, testing for specifications and stability.

PUBLICATIONS

Co-author of Clarification of Ascites Fluid, *Biotechniques.* Volume 10, No. 4 (1991)

CERTIFICATIONS

Maintenance and Trouble Shooting of HP 1100LC and HP GC 6890, Hewlett Packard, 1999 Performing IQ, OQ & PV on instruments, Hewlett Packard, 1999

EDUCATION

BS, Chemistry -University State of New York, 1991

AAS, Chemical Technology - Westchester Community College, 1983

John Smith   212-555-1212

100 Main Street, Anytown, State 12345   e-Mail: jsmith@hotttmail.com

SAMPLE: CHRONOLOGICAL - ONE COMPANY ONLY – DIFFERENT POSITIONS

SUMMARY

Financial executive with extensive experience and proven track record in the pharmaceutical industry. Directed finance reengineering team for the U.S. pharmaceutical business ($3 billion in revenues), which achieved significant improvements in the budgeting process and the monthly financial closing process. Also, led an SAP global finance team, which laid the foundation (common configuration) for successful implementation of SAP as an ERP system. Recognized for accomplishments in reengineering and change management in two recent articles in STRATEGIC FINANCE.

PROFESSIONAL EXPERIENCE

Hoffman-La Roche, Inc. Nutley, NJ   **1977-2000**

Director-Finance Transformation, 1999-2000

- Created a new department with a $950,000 annual budget focused on transforming finance from transition processing to decision and support fostering continuous improvement in the planning process. Designed and implemented job competencies for finance, developed and delivered training
- Programs for the finance and IT, coordinated the Roche North American finance benchmarking process, generated finance wide communications, and assisted the SAP organization in ongoing training.

Director-Finance Reengineering, 1997-1999

- Led a Finance Reengineering initiative utilizing activity based costing which redirected finance activities towards more of a process orientation, customer focus, pro-activity, and business partnering were identified as key attributes.
- Achieved a 50% time saving for management in the planning process resulting in a $5 million cost improvement over two budget cycles.
- Reduced monthly closing cycle from seven days to five days (pre-SAP)

Director Finance Informatics, 1996-1999

- Saved $150,000 annually by outsourcing ongoing maintenance for legacy systems.
- Proactively transitioned selected employees onto SAP enterprise-wide team.

John Smith   **212-555-1212**

SAP Business Process Team Leader-Pharmaceuticals Order Billing Process, 1996-1997
- Generated procedure streamlining enhancement prioritization process.

SAP Global Finance Team Leader-SAP Kernel Upgrade, 1996-1995
- Directed global team in SAP upgrade, resulting in quality, on time, under budget product which met/exceeded all customer requirements.

Director-Customer Financial Services, 1994-1995
- Directed Accounts Payable, Credit and Collections, and Accounts Receivable departments.
- Saved $250,000 annually by outstanding T&E processing to Gelco, reducing T&E audits from %100 to %10, and initiated Imaging for A/P transactions.

Director-Capital Accounting and Financial Analysis, 1993-1994
- Developed initial Capital Expenditure and Procedure Manual which both documented and streamlined the process.
- Created combined local and global Request for Capital Expenditure procedure.

Director Financial Analysis and Corporate Budgeting, 1988-1992
- Coordinated and consolidated strategic plan and budgets and prepared presentations for senior management for Pharmaceuticals, Vitamins and Fine Chemicals, Diagnostics, and Biomedical Laboratories businesses.

Manager-Fixed Asset Accounting,   1984-1987
Manager-Financial Reporting, 1983-1984

Sr. Financial Analyst-Operations Analysis, 1980-1982
Financial Analyst-Project Financial Services, 1977-1980

CERTIFICATION

Licensed as a Certified Public Accountant in New Jersey

EDUCATION
BS, Accounting –St. Peter's College
MBA, – St. Louis University

John Smith   212-555-1212

100 Main Street, Anytown, State 12345   e-Mail: jsmith@hotttmail.com

SAMPLE FUNCTIONAL RESUME

PROFILE

General manager and senior marketing executive with an extensive record of achievement in Fortune 500, leveraged buyout and start-up organization. Produces outstanding results through leadership, strategic vision, organizational development, communication and execution. Experience includes extensive P&L background, business development, new product development turnaround management, mergers, and acquisitions.

ACCOMPLISHMENTS

- In one year, rebuilt a virtually nonexistent new product pipeline for Reckitt & Colman PLC, with winning concepts in development for market introduction over the next three years.
- Developed and launched *Resolve Fabric Refresher* in record time to gain key market position in a new category, generating $35MM in incremental revenue in Year 1.
- Developed and implemented, as part of the executive team, a new corporate infrastructure establishing Personal Care Group, Inc. as a stand-alone company. Reduced overhead by 34% or $7.4MM, versus prior corporate levels.
- Led a newly recruited organization to two years of double-digit increases in operating profit by revitalizing basic product lines and delivering unprecedented new product results in the company's five core businesses.
- Successfully turned around a faltering new product initiative that required investment in an area outside the company's focus and development of a licensed product with 21 SKUs. Secured corporate approval of a three-year investment plan, assembled a cross-functional team and successfully developed, test marketed and launched *Ogilvie* Tender Color hair color on a regional basis.
- Developed and implemented new strategic direction for the base *Ogilvie* Home Permanent business, reversing three-year decline in brand sales and increasing profits by 19%.
- Developed and implemented strategic plan which reversed declining sales volume of Max Factor's Women's Fragrance business and delivered $3.5MM profit for businesses that had previously been unprofitable.
- Positioned and introduced Imari brand, which generated sales of $53MM, 40% above plan, and remains Avon's most successful fragrance entry to date.

John Smith	**212-555-1212**

EXPERIENCE

CRYSTAL JOURNEY CANDLES, LLC, Essex, CT, — 2000-Present
Consultant, Marketing/Business Development

RECKITT & COLMAN PLC, Wayne, NJ, — 1998-1999
Vice President, Marketing, New Products, North America

PERSONAL CARE GROUP, INC., Montvale, NJ, — 1996-1998
Vice President, Marketing

EASTMAN KODAK CP./L&F PRODUCTS, INC., Montvale, NJ, — 1989-1995
Group Product Manager, Personal Products Division

REVLON INC./MAX FACTOR & CO., Stamford, CT,
1985-1989
Director of Marketing, Women's Fragrance

AVON PRODUCTS, INC., New York, NY, — 1978-1985
Senior Product Manager, Women's Fragrance, 1983-1985
Senior Quality Engineer, Corporate Quality Assurance, 1978-1981

YARDLEY OF LONDON, INC., Atlanta, GA, — 1976-1978
Project Leader, Research and Development

NATIONAL SERVICE INDUSTRIES, INC, Atlanta, GA, — 1974-1976
Quality Control Chemist, Research and Development

EDUCATION

B.S. Biology/Chemistry, cum laude, 1974
North Georgia College & State University, Dahlonega, GA

8. Worksheets

Heading

Name: _____

Address: _____

City, State Zip: _____

Phone Number(s): _____

e-Mail Address: _____

Name: _____

Address: _____

City, State Zip: _____

Phone Number(s): _____

e-Mail Address: _____

Name: _____

Address: _____

City, State Zip: _____

Phone Number(s): _____

e-Mail Address: _____

Professional Summary

Work History

_____   _____

(Most Recent Company   City, State)   (Overall Dates Employed)

_____

(One Line Describing Company)

_____   _____

(Position Title)   (Dates)

_____

(One Line Job Description)

- _____

    (OARS Accomplishment - Objective + Action + Result = Statement)

    _____

    _____

    _____

- _____

    (OARS Accomplishment - Objective + Action + Result = Statement)

    _____

    _____

    _____

- _____

    (OARS Accomplishment - Objective + Action + Result = Statement)

    _____

    _____

    _____

- _____

    (OARS Accomplishment - Objective + Action + Result = Statement)

    _____

_____
_____

- _____

  (OARS Accomplishment - Objective + Action + Result = Statement)

  _____
  _____
  _____

- _____

  (OARS Accomplishment - Objective + Action + Result = Statement)

  _____
  _____
  _____

Work History

_____ _____
(Next Company   City, State)   (Overall Dates Employed)
_____
(One Line Describing Company)

_____ _____
(Position Title)   (Dates)
_____
(One Line Job Description)

- _____
(OARS Accomplishment - Objective + Action + Result = Statement)
_____
_____
_____

- _____
(OARS Accomplishment - Objective + Action + Result = Statement)
_____
_____
_____

- _____
(OARS Accomplishment - Objective + Action + Result = Statement)
_____
_____
_____

- _____
(OARS Accomplishment - Objective + Action + Result = Statement)
_____

_____
_____

- _____

  (OARS Accomplishment - Objective + Action + Result = Statement)

  _____
  _____
  _____

- _____

  (OARS Accomplishment - Objective + Action + Result = Statement)

  _____
  _____
  _____

Work History

_____   _____

(Next Company   City, State)   (Overall Dates Employed)

_____

(One Line Describing Company)

_____   _____

(Position Title)   (Dates)

_____

(One Line Job Description)

- _____

    (OARS Accomplishment - Objective + Action + Result = Statement)

    _____

    _____

    _____

- _____

    (OARS Accomplishment - Objective + Action + Result = Statement)

    _____

    _____

    _____

- _____

    (OARS Accomplishment - Objective + Action + Result = Statement)

    _____

    _____

    _____

- _____

    (OARS Accomplishment - Objective + Action + Result = Statement)

    _____

_____
_____

- _____

    (OARS Accomplishment - Objective + Action + Result = Statement)

    _____
    _____
    _____

- _____

    (OARS Accomplishment - Objective + Action + Result = Statement)

    _____
    _____
    _____

Professional Development

_____
(Course Title, Provider)

_____
(Course Title, Provider)

_____
(Course Title, Provider)

_____
(Course Title, Provider)

_____
(Course Title, Provider)

_____
(Course Title, Provider)

_____
(Course Title, Provider)

_____
(Course Title, Provider)

_____
(Course Title, Provider)

_____
(Course Title, Provider)

_____
(Course Title, Provider)

_____
(Course Title, Provider)

Additional Skills

_____

(Examples: Work Related Skills, Learned Computer Skills, Languages, etc.)

_____

(Examples: Work Related Skills, Learned Computer Skills, Languages, etc.)

_____

(Examples: Work Related Skills, Learned Computer Skills, Languages, etc.)

_____

(Examples: Work Related Skills, Learned Computer Skills, Languages, etc.)

_____

(Examples: Work Related Skills, Learned Computer Skills, Languages, etc.)

_____

(Examples: Work Related Skills, Learned Computer Skills, Languages, etc.)

_____

(Examples: Work Related Skills, Learned Computer Skills, Languages, etc.)

_____

(Examples: Work Related Skills, Learned Computer Skills, Languages, etc.)

_____

(Examples: Work Related Skills, Learned Computer Skills, Languages, etc.)

_____

(Examples: Work Related Skills, Learned Computer Skills, Languages, etc.)

_____

(Examples: Work Related Skills, Learned Computer Skills, Languages, etc.)

_____

(Examples: Work Related Skills, Learned Computer Skills, Languages, etc.)

Education

_____

(Degree Awarded, Major Field and School)

_____

(Degree Awarded, Major Field and School)

_____

(Degree Awarded, Major Field and School)

_____

(Degree Awarded, Major Field and School)

_____

(Degree Awarded, Major Field and School)

_____

(Degree Awarded, Major Field and School)

_____

(Degree Awarded, Major Field and School)

_____

(Degree Awarded, Major Field and School)

Associations (Optional)

(Only Business Related Associations that Bring Value to Your Future Employer Through Your Established Relationships)

(Only Business Related Associations that Bring Value to Your Future Employer Through Your Established Relationships)

(Only Business Related Associations that Bring Value to Your Future Employer Through Your Established Relationships)

(Only Business Related Associations that Bring Value to Your Future Employer Through Your Established Relationships)

(Only Business Related Associations that Bring Value to Your Future Employer Through Your Established Relationships)

(Only Business Related Associations that Bring Value to Your Future Employer Through Your Established Relationships)

Other Relevant Data (Optional)

_____

(Awards, Community Leadership, Professional Memberships that Bring Value to Your Future Employer)

_____

(Awards, Community Leadership, Professional Memberships that Bring Value to Your Future Employer)

_____

(Awards, Community Leadership, Professional Memberships that Bring Value to Your Future Employer)

_____

(Awards, Community Leadership, Professional Memberships that Bring Value to Your Future Employer)

NOTES

9. Cover Letters

It is a Cover Letter that you send to a potential employer along with your Resume. A Cover Letter is important because, among other things, (1) it will tell the recipient for whom the Resume is intended, (2) it can elaborate on your knowledge of the company and your desire to work for it, and (3) it allows you to name drop.

Each Cover Letter must be produced for a specific employer. You can recycle some of the text for Cover Letters within the same industry, but each letter should contain a reference to something about the employer/company and what he/she/it has done.

NOTES

10. Cover Letter Template

The Cover Letter Template will show you a standard method to use in creating a Cover Letter for any opportunity. It is broken up into three sections with each section having a specific purpose. In the following page is the Cover Letter Template with each section being described. Your Cover Letters should not exceed one page as anything long usually will not be read by prospective employers.

After The Cover Letter Template, we will see samples of several types of Cover Letter which have produced results for the candidates you have used them for.

The Resume and Cover Letter Writing Toolkit for the $uccessful Job Seeker

Cover Letter Template

Name
Address, Apt. #
City, State Zip
Phone:
FAX:
Email:

Date
Name, Title
Company Name
Address
City, State Zip

Dear Mr. or Ms. XXXXX:

Paragraph 1

- **Mention who you are and why you are contacting their organization.**

Each paragraph should not contain more than 5 to 6 lines. Be short, hard hitting and to the point to capture the reader's attention as soon as possible!

Paragraph 2

- **Mention what you have accomplished for other companies and/or what you can do for their company, based on research you performed about their company.**

Here you should have bulleted statements about your accomplishments (O/A/R/S – Objective/Action/Result = Statement) or what problem you can help the company solving with your background. You want to demonstrate how you can save a company time, money and increase their productivity.

Paragraph 3

- **Call to Action! Here is where you some action to happen!**

In the last paragraph you are thanking the person for their time, requesting an interview, or telling the person you will be calling next week to follow up on this letter.
Sincerely yours,
John Smith
Enc.: Resume

The purpose of the Cover Letter and Resume is not to get you a job but to get you an interview. An interview gets you a job! Keep you letters short and to the point and always demonstrate value – what you can do for them!

11. Sample Cover Letters

John Smith   212-555-1212

---

100 Main Street, Anytown, State 12345   e-Mail: jsmith@hotttmail.com

SAMPLE COVER LETTER

January 1, 2002

Mr. Michael C. Marvis, President
Marvis Construction Company
1121 Jackson Blvd.
Akron, Ohio 24520

Dear Mr. Marvis:

Your recently completed shopping complex on Eighth Avenue is well designed and compatible with the existing neighborhood. I am particularly impressed with how you placed the parking area next to the main access points for the restaurant and theatre complex.

I am especially interested in your work because my background is in architectural drafting. I know good design, and I want to associate with a firm that will fully use my talents. My qualifications include:

- Three years of architectural drafting experience; helped develop plans for $14 million of residential and commercial construction.
- Three years handling all aspects of construction, building and installing cabinets, reconstructing commercial building, pouring concrete.
- Collected and evaluated data for controlling quality of construction.
- Trained as a draftsman.

At present I am seeking an opportunity to use my skills in developing projects similar to your Eighth Avenue shopping complex.

I would appreciate an opportunity to meet with you to discuss our mutual interests. I will call your office next week to arrange a convenient time.

I look forward to meeting you.

Sincerely yours,

John Smith

The Resume and Cover Letter Writing Toolkit for the $uccessful Job Seeker

John Smith   212-555-1212

100 Main Street, Anytown, State 12345   e-Mail: jsmith@hotttmail.com

SAMPLE COVER LETTER

January 1, 2002

Mr. Michael C. Marvis, President
Marvis Construction Company
1121 Jackson Blvd.
Akron, Ohio 24520

Dear Mr. Marvis:

In today's competitive climate in the banking industry, one of the most important resources a bank can have is a staff member well qualified in the area of Customer Relations – not only to attract new customers, but also to retain those already on board. My background and experience make me uniquely fitted for such a position.

In the past fifteen years, at Chase Manhattan Bank, I have effectively supervised and managed twelve branches. My accomplishments include the following:

- $250,000 in money market fund sales over 9-month period.
- Weekly sales of 10-15 certificates of deposit.
- Resolution of 99% of all customer complaints to the satisfaction of both bank and customer.
- Solution of numerous operational problems to everyone's satisfaction.
- Minimal loss of money in seven hold-ups involving four branches; major factor was compliance by staff to my security instructions.

I would welcome the opportunity to discuss with you how my experience and abilities might make a substantial contribution to your operation. With that in mind I will call your office next week to arrange a mutually convenient time for us to meet.

Very truly yours,

John Smith

John Smith   212-555-1212

100 Main Street, Anytown, State 12345   e-Mail: jsmith@hotttmail.com

SAMPLE COVER LETTER

January 1, 2002

Mr. Michael C. Marvis, President
Marvis Construction Company
1121 Jackson Blvd.
Akron, Ohio 24520

Dear Mr. Marvis:

    Advanced Technology's word processing equipment is the finest on the market today. I know, because I have used different systems over the past eight years. Your company is the type of organization I would like to be associated with.

    Over the next few months I will be seeking a sales position with an information processing company. My technical, sales, and administrative experience include:

- **Technical:** Eight years operating Mag card and high-speed printers: IBM 6240, Mag A, I, II, IBM 6640, and Savin word processor.
- **Sales:** Recruited clients; maintained inventory; received and filled orders; improved business-community relations.
- **Administrative:** Planned and re-organized word processing center; created new tracking and filing system; initiated time and cost studies which reduced labor costs by $30,000 and improved efficiency of operations.

    In addition, I have a Bachelor's degree in communication with emphasis on public speaking, interpersonal communication, and psychology.

    Your company interests me very much. I would appreciate an opportunity to meet with you to discuss how my qualifications can best meet your needs. Therefore, I will call your office next Monday, January 18, to arrange a meeting with you at a convenient time.

Thank you for your time and consideration.

Sincerely,

John Smith

The Resume and Cover Letter Writing Toolkit for the $uccessful Job Seeker

John Smith 212-555-1212

100 Main Street, Anytown, State 12345 e-Mail: jsmith@hotttmail.com

SAMPLE COVER LETTER

Response to Advertisement (Best Response Rate!)

January 1, 2002
Mr. Michael C. Marvis, President
Marvis Construction Company
1121 Jackson Blvd.
Akron, Ohio 24520
Dear Mr. Marvis:

Your advertisement in the New York Times, on June 9, 2002, for an Assessment Coordinator seems to perfectly match my background and experience. As the International Brand Coordinator for Kahlua, I coordinated meetings, prepared presentations and materials, organized a major off-site conference, and supervised an assistant. I believe that I am an excellent candidate for this position as I have illustrated below:

YOUR REQUIREMENTS	MY QUALIFICATIONS
A highly motivated, diplomatic, flexible, quality-driven professional	Successfully managed project teams involving different business units. The defined end results were achieved on every project.
Exceptional organizational skills and attention to detail	Planned the development and launch of the Kahula Heritage Edition bottle series. My former manager enjoyed leaving the "details" and follow-through to me. Attended Coverdale project management training.
College degree and minimum 3 years relevant business experience	B.A. from Vassar College (1994). 5+ years business experience in productive, professional environments.
Computer literacy	Extensive knowledge of Windows & Macintosh Applications.

I am interested in this position because it fits well with my new career focus in the human resources field. Currently, I am enrolled in NYU's adult career planning and development certificate program and working at Lee Hecht Harrison.

I have enclosed my resume to provide more information on my strengths and career achievements. If after reviewing my material you believe that there is a match, please call me. Thank you for your consideration.
Sincere regards,
John Smith

12. Conclusion

In this document you have learn the purpose of the Resume, that is, to get you an interview and the interview gets you the job. Most Resumes are only reviewed for about 10 to 14 seconds, so it is important that your Resume be clear, concise, easy-to-read and demonstrate your accomplishments.

You have also learned about using **Action Verbs** in your accomplishment statements. Accomplishment statements should have the **OARS (Objective + Action + Result = Statement)** format built into them.

Components of the Resume discusses the various sections of the Resume and their purpose. There are five main sections of the Resume:

Heading

Summary

Work History with Achievements

Professional Development/Additional Skills

Education

Posting your Resume on the Internet is one of the methods of being found by prospective employers and executive recruiters for jobs that they are looking to fill. Some sample Resume posting sites are in the section **"If You Want to Post Your Resume"**.

You have learned how to prepare an effective Resume that prospective employers and executive recruiters like to use when interviewing potential candidates for employment opportunities. Refer to this manual often to fine tune your Resume as your work situation changes.

Now go out there and get the job of your dreams, armed with your well prepared, results demonstrating Resume and show your next employer you can make a difference to their bottom line!

13. If You Want to Post Your Resume

Posting your Resume on the Internet is one of the ways to get your credentials in front of potential employers and recruiters. You may want to also investigate search engines like Google (www.google.com) and Yahoo (www.yahoo.com) and look at their directories for "Business - Jobs" section as job web sites come and go.

One suggestion is to post your Resume on industry specific web sites. For instance, if you are in computer industry you might want to post your Resume on ComputerJobs.com (www.computerjobs.com). There are also general purpose web sites as well like The Monster Board (www.monster.com) and HotJobs (www.hotjobs.com).

Some web sites (www.geocites.com and www.tripod.com) offer you a free or low cost method to have your own web page. You can post your Resume on your own web site so you can be found. One word of caution is that your personal information will be viewed by everyone so you might want to exercise some caution.

There are hundreds of web sites to post your Resume. Below are only a small sampling of Resume posting web sites.

Resume Posting Web Sites
www.monster.com
www.careerbuilder.com
www.hotjobs.com
www.headhunter.net
www.careermag.com
www.careermart.com
www.computerjobs.com
www.hrjobs.com
www.salesjobs.com
www.engineeringjobs.com
www.hire.com

NOTES